SCHIRMER PERFORMANCE EDITIONS

BEETHOVEN

PIANO SONATA NO. 29
IN B-FLAT MAJOR
Opus 106 ("Hammerklavier")

Edited and Recorded by Robert Taub

Also Available:
BEETHOVEN PIANO SONATAS
edited and recorded by Robert Taub

Volume I, Nos. 1–15
00296632 Book only
00296634 CDs only (5 disc set)

Volume II, Nos. 16–32
00296633 Book only
00296635 CDs only (5 disc set)

On the cover:
The Tree of Crows, 1822 (oil on canvas)
by Caspar David Friedrich
(1774–1840)
© Louvre, Paris, France/Giraudon/The Bridgeman Art Library

ISBN 978-1-4768-1638-8

G. SCHIRMER, Inc.

DISTRIBUTED BY

HAL•LEONARD®
CORPORATION
7777 W. BLUEMOUND RD. P.O. BOX 13819 MILWAUKEE, WI 53213

www.schirmer.com
www.halleonard.com

CONTENTS

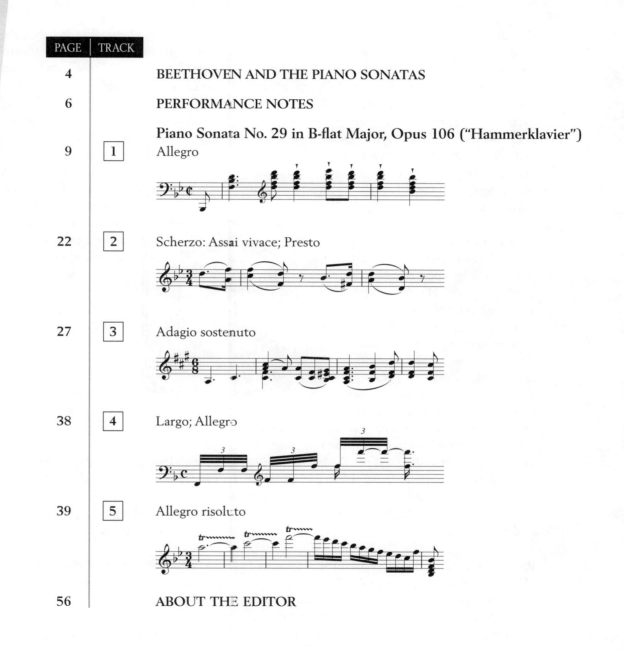

BEETHOVEN
AND THE PIANO SONATAS

In 1816, Beethoven wrote to his friend and admirer Carl Czerny: "You must forgive a composer who would rather hear his work just as he had written it, however beautifully you played it otherwise." Having lost patience with Czerny's excessive interpolations in the piano part of a performance of Beethoven's *Quintet for Piano and Winds*, Op. 16, Beethoven also addressed the envelope sarcastically to "Herr von Zerni, celebrated virtuoso." On all levels, Beethoven meant what he wrote.

As a composer who bridged the gulf between court and private patronage on one hand (the world of Bach, Handel, Haydn, and Mozart) and on the other hand earning a living based substantially on sales of printed works and/or public perform- ances (the world of Brahms), Beethoven was one of the first composers to become almost obsessively concerned with the accuracy of his published scores. He often bemoaned the seeming unending streams of mistakes. "Fehler—fehler!— Sie sind selbst ein einziger Fehler" ("Mistakes— mistakes!—You yourselves are a unique mistake") he wrote to the august publishing firm of Breitkopf und Härtel in 1811.

It is not surprising, therefore, that toward the end of his life Beethoven twice (1822 and again in 1825) begged his publishers C.F. Peters and Schott to bring out a comprehensive complete edition of his works over which Beethoven himself would have editorial control, and would thus be able to ensure accuracy in all dimensions—notes, pedaling and fingering, expressive notations (dynamics, slurs), and articulations, and even movement headings. This never happened.

Beethoven was also obsessive about his musical sketches that he kept with him throughout his mature life. Desk sketchbooks, pocket sketch- books: thousands of pages reveal his innermost compositional musings, his labored processes of creativity, the ideas that he abandoned, and the many others—often jumbled together—that he crafted through dint of extraordinary determi- nation, single-minded purpose, and the inspiration of genius into works that endure all exigencies of time and place. In the autograph scores that Beethoven then sent on to publishers, further layers of the creative processes abound. But even these scores might not be the final word in a particular work; there are instances in which Beethoven made textual changes, additions, or deletions by way of letters to publishers, corrections to proofs, and/or post-publication changes to first editions.

We can appreciate the unique qualities of the Beethoven piano sonatas on many different levels. Beethoven's own relationship with these works was fundamentally different from his relationship to his works of other genres. The early sonatas served as vehicles for the young Beethoven as both composer and pianist forging his path in Vienna, the musical capital of Europe at that time. Throughout his compositional lifetime, even when he no longer performed publicly as a pianist, Beethoven used his thirty-two piano sonatas as crucibles for all manner of musical ideas, many of which he later re-crafted—often in a distilled or more rarefied manner—in the sixteen string quartets and the nine symphonies.

The pianoforte was evolving at an enormous rate during the last years of the eighteenth century extending through the first several decades of the nineteenth. As a leading pianist and musical figure of his day, Beethoven was in the vanguard of this technological development. He was not content to confine his often explosive playing to the smaller sonorous capabilities of the instruments he had on hand; similarly, his compositions demanded more from the pianofortes of the day—greater depth of sonority, more subtle levels of keyboard finesse and control, and increased registral range.

These sonatas themselves pushed forward further development and technical innovation from the piano manufacturers.

Motivating many of the sonatas are elements of extraordinary—even revolutionary—musical experimentation extending into domains of form, harmonic development, use of the instrument, and demands placed upon the performer, the piano, and the audience. However, the evolution of these works is not a simple straight line.

I believe that the usual chronological groupings of "early," "middle," and "late" are too superficial for Beethoven's piano sonatas. Since he composed more piano sonatas than substantial works of any other single genre (except songs) and the period of composition of the piano sonatas extends virtually throughout Beethoven's entire creative life, I prefer chronological groupings derived from more specific biographical and stylistic considerations. I delve into greater depth on this and other aspects of the sonatas in my book *Playing the Beethoven Piano Sonatas* (Amadeus Press).

1795–1800: Sonatas Op. 2 no. 1, Op. 2 no. 2, Op. 2 no. 3, Op. 7, Op. 10 no. 1, Op. 10 no. 2, Op. 10 no. 3, Op. 13, Op. 14 no. 1, Op. 14 no. 2, Op. 22, Op. 49 no. 1, Op. 49 no. 2

1800–1802: Sonatas Op. 26, Op. 27 no. 1, Op. 27 no. 2, Op. 28, Op. 31 no. 1, Op. 31 no. 2, Op. 31 no. 3

1804: Sonatas Op. 53, Op. 54, Op. 57

1809: Sonatas Op. 78, Op. 79, Op. 81a

1816–1822: Sonatas Op. 90, Op. 101, Op. 106, Op. 109, Op. 110, Op. 111

From 1804 (post-Heiligenstadt) forward, there were no more multiple sonata opus numbers; each work was assigned its own opus. Beethoven no longer played in public, and his relationship with the sonatas changed subtly.

—*Robert Taub*

PERFORMANCE NOTES

Extracted from *Beethoven: Piano Sonatas Volume II*, edited by Robert Taub.

For the preparation of this edition, I have consulted autograph scores, first editions, and sketchbooks whenever possible. (Complete autograph scores of only twelve of the piano sonatas—plus the autograph of only the first movement of Sonata Op. 81a—have survived.) I have also read Beethoven's letters with particular attention to his many remarks concerning performances of his day and the lists of specific changes/corrections that he sent to publishers. We all know—as did Beethoven—that musical notation is imperfect, but it is the closest representation we have to the artistic ideal of a composer. We strive to represent that ideal as thoroughly and accurately as possible.

Tempo

My recordings of these sonatas are available as companions to the two published volumes. I have also included my suggestions for tempo (metronome markings) for each sonata, at the beginning of each movement.

Fingering

I have included Beethoven's own fingering suggestions. His fingerings—intended not only for himself (in earlier sonatas) but primarily for successive generations of pianists—often reveal intensely musical intentions in their shaping of musical contour and molding of the hands to create specific musical textures. I have added my own fingering suggestions, all of which are aimed at creating meaningful musical constructs. As a general guide, I believe in minimizing hand motions as much as possible, and therefore many of my fingering suggestions are based on the pianist's hands proceeding in a straight line as long as musically viable and physically practicable. I also believe that the pianist can develop senses of tactile feeling for specific musical patterns.

Pedaling

I have also included Beethoven's pedal markings in this edition. These indications are integral parts of the musical fabric. However, since most often no pedal indication is offered, whenever necessary one should use the right pedal—sparingly and subtly—to help achieve legato playing as well as to enhance sonorities.

Ornamentation

My suggestions regarding ornamental turns concern the notion of keeping the contour smooth while providing an expressive musical gesture with an increased sense of forward direction. The actual starting note of a turn depends on the specific context: if it is preceded by the same note (as in Sonata Op. 10 no. 2, second movement, m. 42), then I would suggest that the turn is four notes, starting on the upper neighbor: upper neighbor, main note, lower neighbor, main note.

Sonata in F Major, Opus 10 no. 2:
second movement, m. 42, r.h.

However, if the turn is preceded by another note (as in Sonata Op. 10 no. 2, first movement, m. 38), then the turn could be five notes in total, starting on the main note: main note, upper neighbor, main note, lower neighbor, main note.

Sonata in F Major, Opus 10 no. 2:
first movement, m. 38, r.h.

Whenever Beethoven included an afterbeat (Nachschlag) for a trill, I have included it as well. When he did not, I have not added any.

Footnotes

Footnotes within the musical score offer contextual explanations and alternatives based on earlier representations of the music (first editions, autograph scores) that Beethoven had seen and corrected. In areas where specific markings are visible only in the autograph score, I explain the reasons and context for my choices of musical representation. Other footnotes are intended to clarify ways of playing specific ornaments.

Notes on the Sonata[1]

PIANO SONATA NO. 29 IN B-FLAT MAJOR, OPUS 106 ("Hammerklavier") (1817–18)

Sonata Op. 106 is the longest of the Beethoven sonatas, infrequently played because of its extreme interpretive and pianistic challenges. Having lived with the "Hammerklavier" for eight years before performing it publicly for the first time, learning and relearning, experimenting, and then playing it in many concerts and recording it, I have come to relish its challenges, and realize that to play it well, concentration of total immersion is required.

In the **Allegro**, dramatic tension is engendered by a fundamental clash between the tonalities of B-flat major and B major (and B minor). The very opening of this movement is undeniably treacherous; particularly at tempo, it is easily possible to miss one of the notes of the chord. I make sure both hands are in position before beginning, and then look at the area of the keyboard of the first left-hand chord. Wherever the eyes are, the hand is sure to follow.

Every principal theme is closely related to this opening one, which is motivated by the interval of a third in both rising and descending gestures. (Every one of the five movements of this sonata is constructed with large-scale trajectories of descending thirds, as well as with themes whose principal motivating characteristic is the interval of the third.) The fermata over the quarter rest in m. 4 allows the reverberations of the enormous opening to dissipate and gives the performer time to prepare for the *piano* dynamic and legato touch of the melodic line that fills in the opening thirds. In m. 15, I make sure that the left-hand dynamic, even within the crescendo, does not overpower the intrepid right hand as it reaches to the top of the keyboard.

The development of the opening thematic motive is thorough and consuming. I make sure to begin the fugue quietly (m. 137) and in a very steady rhythm, a strict pulse of four beats per bar. This feeling exemplifies a sense of "working out" of the motive. In m. 201, the touch is again very different.

I play the beginning of the B major area with very curved, intense fingers (as opposed to the flatter fingers in the previous four measures) to produce direct but thinner qualities of sound.

An infamous textual controversy in the Allegro concerns the area of the transition to the recapitulation (mm. 224-226). Within the key signature of B Major (five sharps), Beethoven did not mark a natural sign in front of each A (eight of them), and yet there is an argument that he meant to, but just forgot. An Artaria first edition in the Scheide collection has only the A (sharps), no natural signs. In the letters to Ries of the 20 March and 16 April 1819—those in which Beethoven detailed more than one hundred other corrections—he made no mention of this passage. Consistent with the nature of the movement and the expressive function of this transistion, the tritone of A-sharp-E generates far more tension than the bare fourth of A-E. Furthermore and perhaps most convincing, the recapitulation begins with a B-flat octave, not just a low B-flat note as in every other statement of this motive—the tenor B-flat is an enharmonic reinterpretation of the A-sharp that preceded it. The octave B-flat is also the reason that it is necessary to have a triple D in the left hand in m. 229; for the music's trajectory to continue, the third of the triad (rather than the root) is stressed. For all these reasons, I play A-sharps here.

In the recapitulation, the secondary theme is in G-flat major rather than in G major as it is in the exposition. The trill beginning in m. 338 is the only trill I know of in the entire literature that is surrounded by octaves in the same hand; I use the only fingering possible—2-3—except for m. 340, in which I use 1-2. Regardless of the quick tempo, it is important to allow the stark contrasts between *forte* and *piano* in the coda to be felt, as the G-flat—F-sharp tension resurfaces. Similarly, the pedal markings in the last five measures are very specific and help establish a rhythmic trajectory which, along with the progression of F–D–B-flat as the uppermost notes heard in the penultimate two bars, concludes the movement powerfully in B-flat major.

The **Scherzo: Assai vivace** second movement is much smaller in formal scope than the first movement. Repeating the top notes of each hand in the upbeat and downbeat figures is a challenge at the intended tempo. A piano adjusted for a large

1 Excerpted from *Playing the Beethoven Piano Sonatas* by Robert Taub
  edited and abridged by Susanne Sheston
  © 2002 by Robert Taub
  Published by Amadeus Press
  Used by permission.

degree of aftertouch can be more responsive. Even so, I play the upbeats lightly, barely depressing the keys, so that the downbeat can be played with slightly more force. I begin the Presto area with a quarter-note pulse that is slightly faster than that of the previous music. Although the touch is light, the tempo cannot be too much faster if the offbeat right-hand chords beginning in m. 89 are to be clear. In mm. 106–112, I drop in dynamics for the prestissimo ascending run, which is light and gives the effect of being simply tossed off.

The **Adagio sostenuto** is among the longest and most dramatic slow movements that Beethoven composed in any genre. I keep an inner pulse of six beats per bar to avoid playing in a slow duple pulse. When the main theme begins to recur in m. 27, the left pedal is lifted as indicated by *tutte le corde*. I change the right pedal with every sixteenth note to avoid pedaling through the left-hand rests and negating their expressive qualities. As the surface motion slows considerably in m. 57, I make sure to maintain an even pulse to guard against rushing, allowing the harmonies their full due. In the area following the greatest emotional intensity, beginning in m. 107, Beethoven's expressive terms imply spaciousness of expression. Large registral spans in m. 118 and m. 121 also broaden the music physically (for the player) and aurally as well.

In no other Beethoven piano work are there more *una corda* and *tre corde* markings. These directives for the use of the left pedal relate not only to quantity of sound (soft vs. loud) but perhaps more importantly to quality of sound. A pianissimo sound can be more present if the strings are struck normally (*tre corde*) by the hammers, or it can seem more distant if the left pedal is depressed (*una corda*). Hence, the placement of *una corda* in m. 61 (and m. 145) has more to do with subtle timbral differences that come into play when the left pedal is depressed than with quantity of sound, since the dynamic is already very soft. The connection between the decreasing dynamics of the final two chords and Beethoven's *tre corde* indication—which may initially seem contradictory—is critically focused upon timbre.

I do not wait any longer than the silence of the last eighth rest of the Adagio before beginning the **Largo**. This movement is an improvisatory link between the Adagio and the Allegro risoluto. I begin each new theme somewhat tentatively, as if seeking the right path, but with the arrival of the third theme (G-sharp minor, m. 3) and its establishment of a more definite meter, we can feel as though we have finally found our way.

Although the chain of trills that begins the **Allegro risoluto** seems improvisatory, it is not and should not be played that way. The trills lead, with a direct and strong bass underpinning, to the theme which forms the basis for the entire fugal last movement. Although the entire movement has only one ritardando indication, I do allow the music to breathe, taking time to resolve cadences.

There is not much time for long trills in the intense stretto of mm. 233–236. In fact, just a short trill of three or five notes is sufficient; the main idea is a concentration on the leaps of a tenth, and the trill is simply a thematic reminder. The choralelike variation that follows is wholly unexpected and is played with a solemn and steady grace. Following the poco adagio, which serves notice that the end is near, *pianissimo* thematic fragments— played clearly and back in tempo—lead to the opening motive back in octaves in both hands. So interwoven is the emphasis on thirds that even the coda avoids a V–I cadence until the very end. Of course, I play these chords *fortissimo*, but I elongate the eighth rest before the penultimate chord by just a fraction of a second, giving the final cadence a little more drama and weight.

It is no secret that Beethoven became convinced of the necessity of metronome markings during the last decade of his life. The "Hammerklavier" is the only Sonata for which he ascribed metronome markings; that such markings should remain largely unrespected today is puzzling. It has been shown that Beethoven's metronome was not faulty, and that he took seriously the setting of tempi. It must be assumed that his metronome markings accurately reflect his hearing of the piece in his inner ear. Although pianists to this day have considered the metronome markings of this piece to be unplayable—too fast—except for the Largo, I disagree. Since Beethoven worked on Op. 106 for almost two full years and was fully immersed in its musical universe, for him the tempos were not unduly fast. True, they stretch the limits of pianism, but the work stretches the limits of musical perceptions on many levels.

Dedicated to Archduke Rudolph

Sonata in B-flat Major
(Sonate für das Hammerklavier)

Ludwig van Beethoven
Opus 106
Composed 1817–1818

a) The metronome markings, pedal markings, and fingering in italics are Beethoven's.

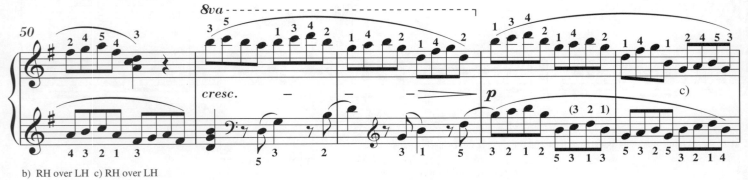

b) RH over LH c) RH over LH

d) RH over LH e) The autograph of Op. 106 remains lost. The placement of slurs in the first edition is unclear here; both the RH and LH slurs may extend across the barline, linking mm. 61–62 with m. 63. f) No middle voice in the first edition. The C–E is occasionally suggested as a possible voice "for consistency," but the sound is more brilliant without them.

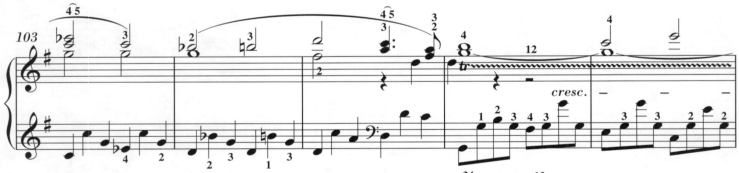

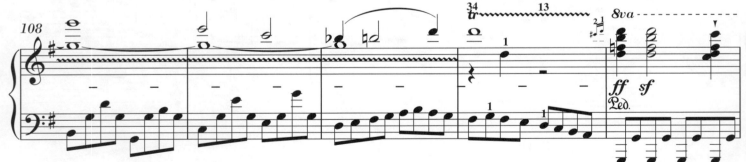

g) This notation, assuming it faithfully depicts the autograph, represents aspects of Beethoven's manner of playing. h) These slurs (mm. 149, 151, 164, 168–172) are not in the first edition. I have followed later editions here.

i) The Artaria edition does not include these sharps before these Gs in m. 210 and m. 212; however, the first English edition does. See Performance Notes.

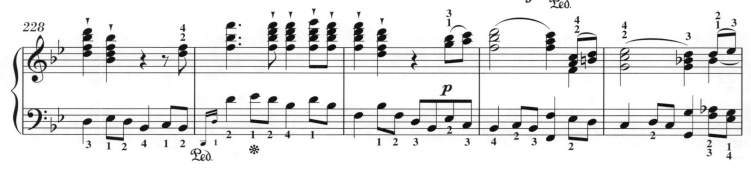

j) I believe A-sharp to be correct here. See Performance Notes.

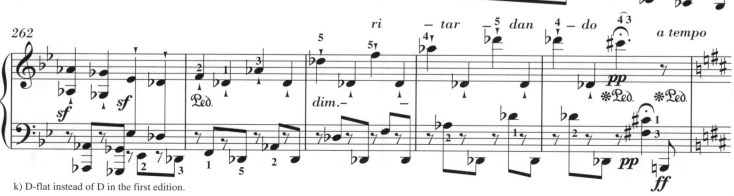

k) D-flat instead of D in the first edition.

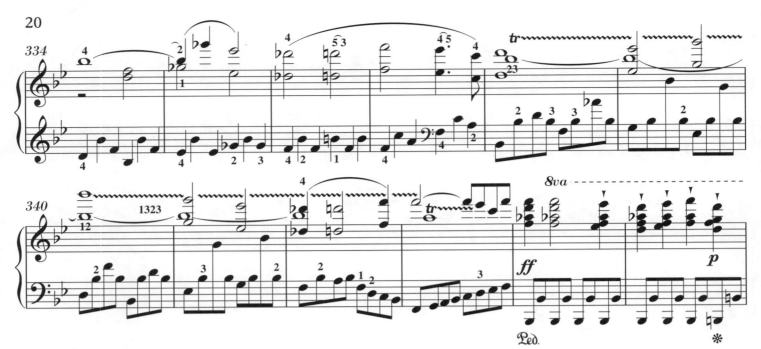

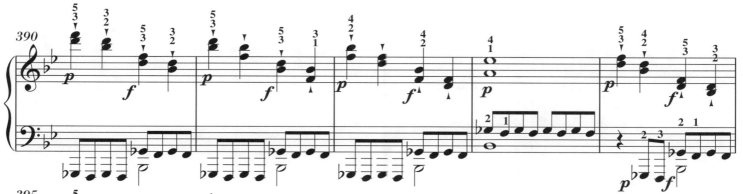

SCHERZO
Assai vivace ♩. = 80

l) This B-flat is not present in the first edition.

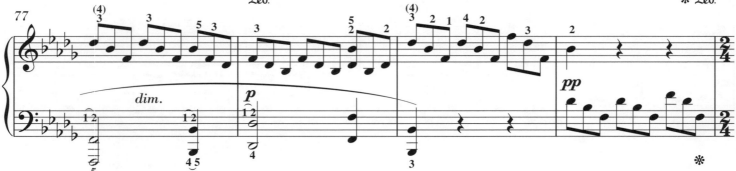

Prestissimo

112

Tempo I

dolce

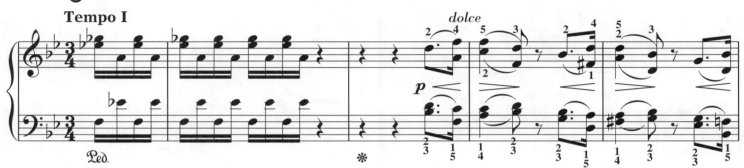

117

122

127

132

Adagio sostenuto ♪ = 92
Appassionato e con molto sentimento

una corda mezza voce

poco cresc. *cresc.*

p

cresc. *p*

espressivo *tutte le corde* *p* *cresc.*

m) As per the first edition. Several later editions have an A-sharp here.

n) As per first edition; some later editions leave out the A in the bass.

o) Not present on Beethoven's piano. I play only the top C-sharp here.

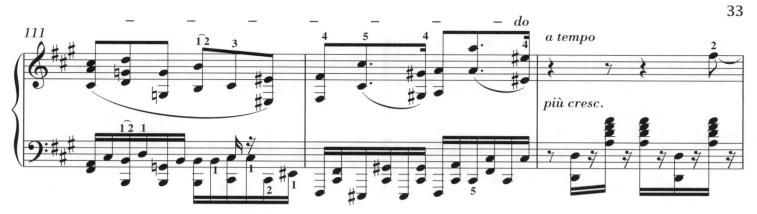

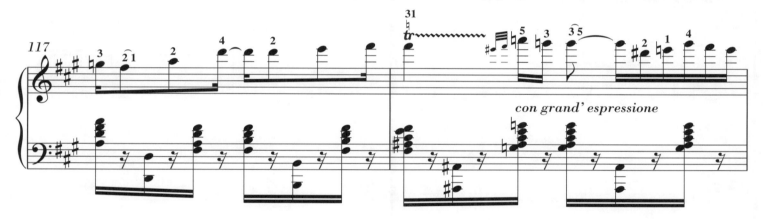

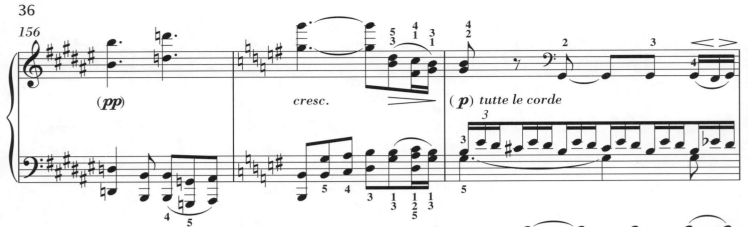

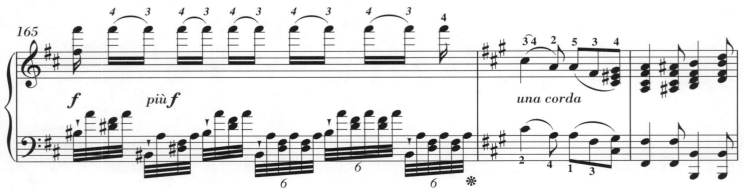

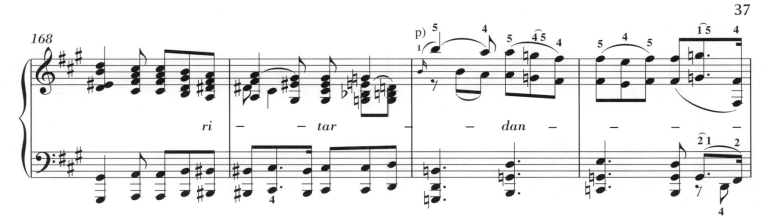

p) As per the first edition. Later editions print a G here as an appoggiatura.   q) In the first edition there are no ties here.   r) See Performance Notes.

Per la misura si conta nel largo sempre quattro semicrome, cio è ♪ ♪ ♪ ♪

Largo ♪ = 76

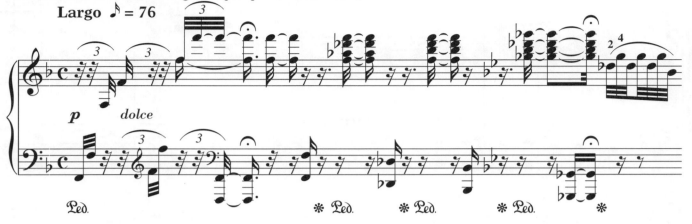

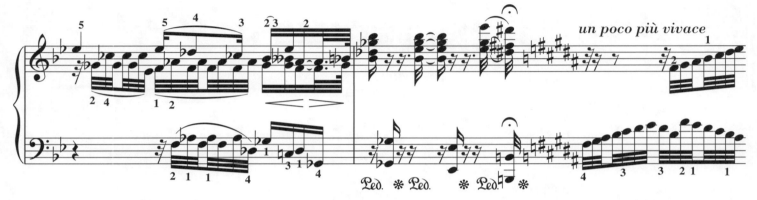

un poco più vivace

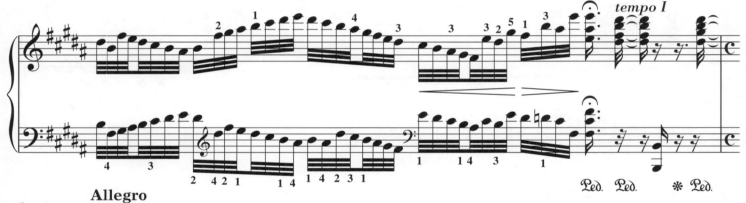

tempo I

Allegro

s) tempo I

s) As per the first edition. Later editions print ❜⋯.

t) The trill is of primary motivic importance, but the Nachschlag (tail) is not. Consequently these are instances in which Beethoven did not include the Nachschlag.

u) In the first edition there are no accidentals in front of the E-flats in mm. 33 and 35. Subsequent editions have natural signs. I believe E-flat is correct.

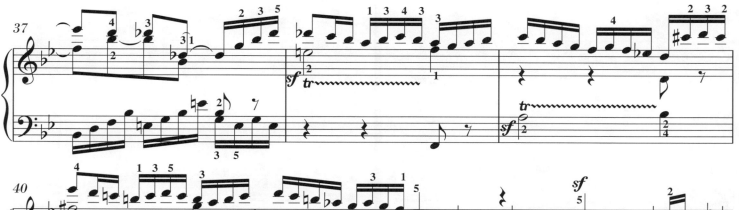

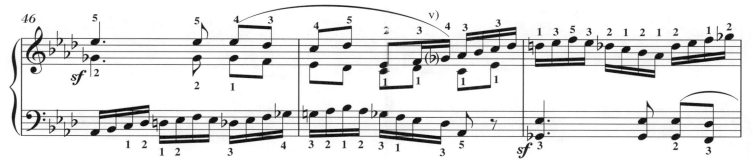

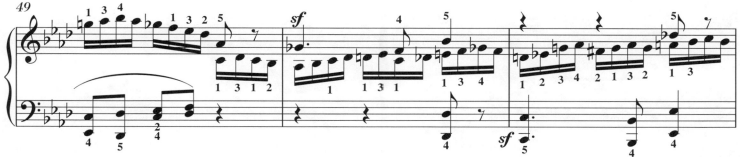

v) No flat in the first edition. G-flat is consistent with the intervallic complexion of the theme.

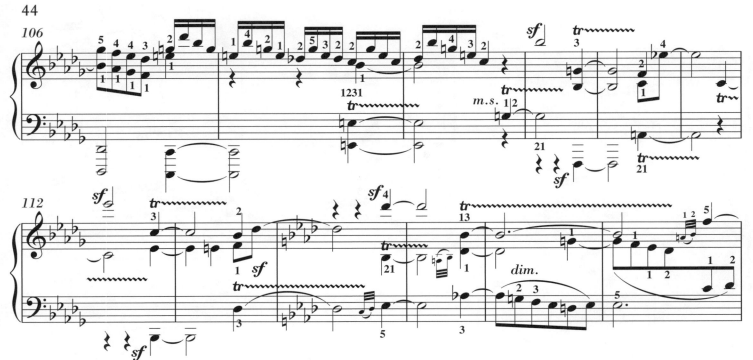

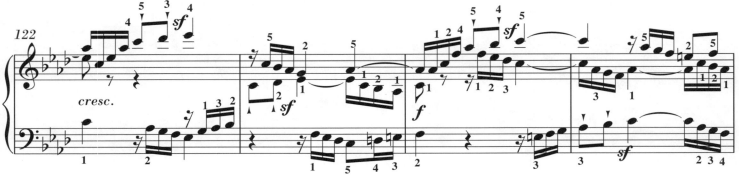

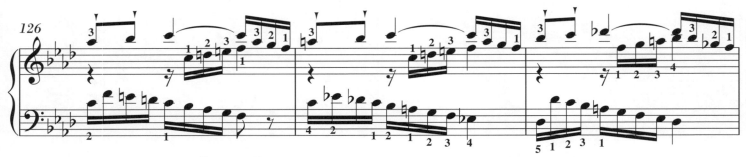

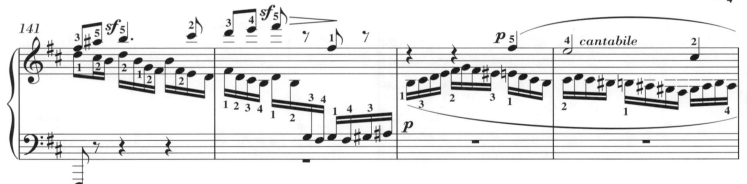

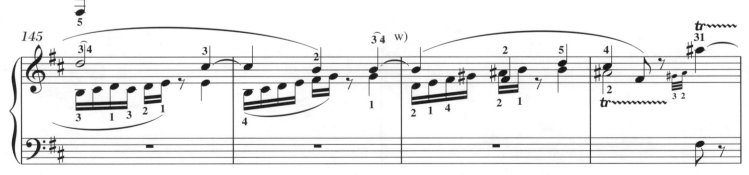

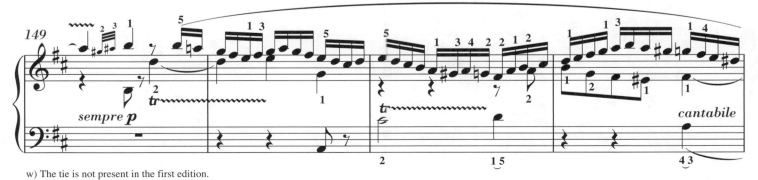

w) The tie is not present in the first edition.

46

x) The tie linking the Ds is not present in the first edition.

y) RH

z) The natural signs in front of the Cs are not present in the first edition, but some subsequent editions print them. I believe that C-sharps are correct here.

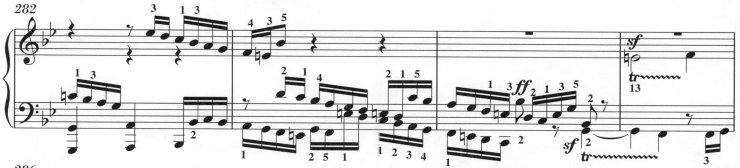

sempre ben marcato

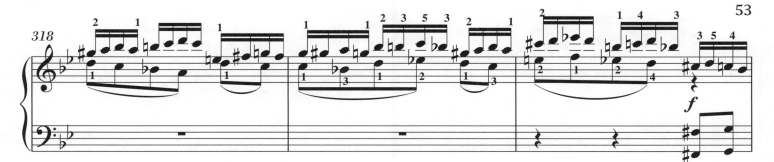

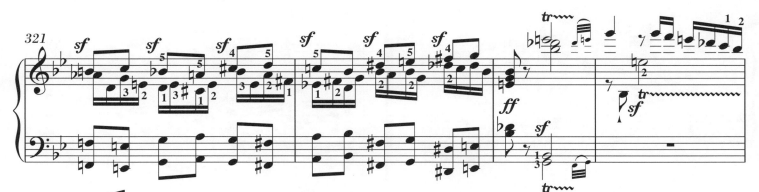

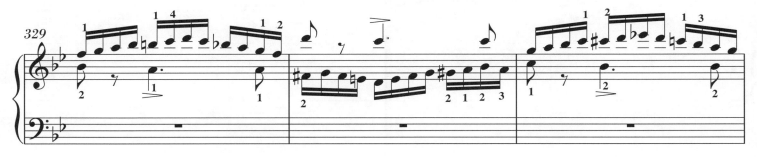

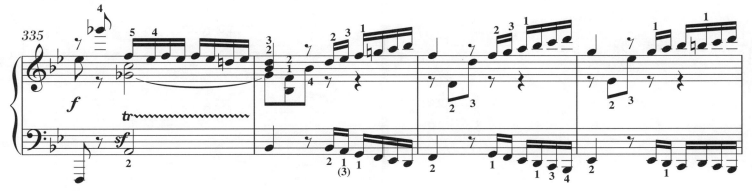

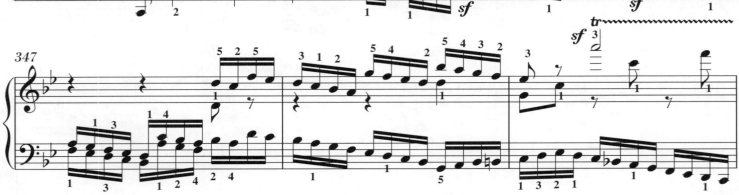

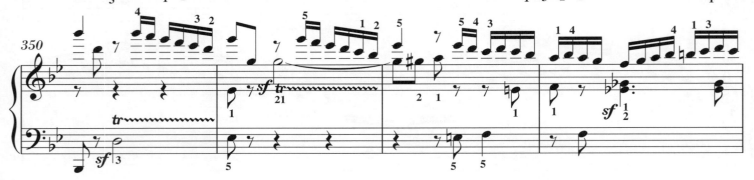

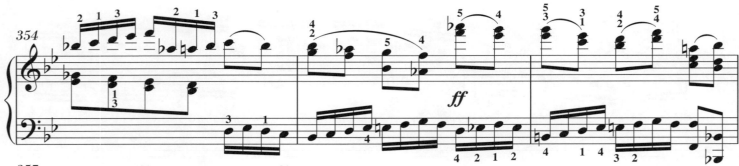

ABOUT THE EDITOR

Robert Taub

From New York's Carnegie Hall to Hong Kong's Cultural Centre to Germany's *avant garde* Zentrum für Kunst und Medientechnologie, Robert Taub is acclaimed internationally. He has performed as soloist with the MET Orchestra in Carnegie Hall, the Boston Symphony Orchestra, BBC Philharmonic, The Philadelphia Orchestra, San Francisco Symphony, Los Angeles Philharmonic, Montreal Symphony, Munich Philharmonic, Orchestra of St. Luke's, Hong Kong Philharmonic, Singapore Symphony, and others.

Robert Taub has performed solo recitals on the Great Performers Series at New York's Lincoln Center and other major series worldwide. He has been featured in international festivals, including the Saratoga Festival, the Lichfield Festival in England, San Francisco's Midsummer Mozart Festival, the Geneva International Summer Festival, among others.

Following the conclusion of his highly celebrated New York series of Beethoven Piano Sonatas, Taub completed a sold-out Beethoven cycle in London at Hampton Court Palace. His recordings of the complete Beethoven Piano Sonatas have been praised throughout the world for their insight, freshness, and emotional involvement. In addition to performing, Robert Taub is an eloquent spokesman for music, giving frequent engaging and informal lectures and pre-concert talks. His book on Beethoven—*Playing the Beethoven Piano Sonatas*—has been published internationally by Amadeus Press.

Taub was featured in a recent PBS television program—*Big Ideas*—that highlighted him playing and discussing Beethoven Piano Sonatas. Filmed during his time as Artist-in-Residence at the Institute for Advanced Study, this program has been broadcast throughout the US on PBS affiliates.

Robert Taub's performances are frequently broadcast on radio networks around the world, including the NPR (Performance Today), Ireland's RTE, and Hong Kong's RTHK. He has also recorded the Sonatas of Scriabin and works of Beethoven, Schumann, Liszt, and Babbitt for Harmonia Mundi, several of which have been selected as "critic's favorites" by *Gramophone*, *Newsweek*, *The New York Times*, *The Washington Post*, *Ovation*, and *Fanfare*.

Robert Taub is involved with contemporary music as well as the established literature, premiering piano concertos by Milton Babbitt (MET Orchestra, James Levine) and Mel Powell (Los Angeles Philharmonic), and making the first recordings of the Persichetti Piano Concerto (Philadelphia Orchestra, Charles Dutoit) and Sessions Piano Concerto. He has premiered six works of Milton Babbitt (solo piano, chamber music, Second Piano Concerto). Taub has also collaborated with several 21st-century composers, including Jonathan Dawe (USA), David Bessell (UK), and Ludger Brümmer (Germany) performing their works in America and Europe.

Taub is a Phi Beta Kappa graduate of Princeton where he was a University Scholar. As a Danforth Fellow he completed his doctoral degree at The Juilliard School where he received the highest award in piano. Taub has served as Artist-in-Residence at Harvard University, at UC Davis, as well as at the Institute for Advanced Study. He has led music forums at Oxford and Cambridge Universities and The Juilliard School. Taub has also been Visiting Professor at Princeton University and at Kingston University (UK).